THE POWER OF
BE that!

Empowering You to Transform Your Essence

Dr. Roneisha Monyette Randall, B.S. Ed.D.

Published by Fina Press, an imprint of WoW Media Publishing

www.wowmediapublishing.com
Facebook: @wowmediapublishingFB
Instagram: @wowmediapublishinglm

ISBN: (Paperback) 978-1-963998-02-3
ISBN: (E-Pub) 978-1-963998-03-0

Cover design by: Heidi Sutherlin, My Creative Pursuits

Library of Congress Control Number: 2024905534

1 2 3 4 5 6 7 8 LSI 29 28 27 26 25 24 23

DEDICATION

To my family and loved ones, who have given me their unwavering love and support, thank you. You all are truly answered prayers and your love is felt profoundly. I love you deeply.

To my dearest father, who I so desperately wish could be here in the physical realm. Thank you for the love and example of fatherhood you showed me while you were living. So much of me is you. I'm grateful to have been your baby girl.

Lastly, this book is dedicated to every individual who wakes up with the certainty that they were destined for more, who refuses to let mediocrity be their resting place, who are prepared to embrace their purpose, unafraid to walk in boldness, who uses their life experiences as lessons not failures, those who are prepared to assert their faith over their fears, knowing that their best is yet to come. May these pages ignite an eternal flame within you that never dims.

With All My Love,

Dr. Roneisha M. Randall (Dr. Ro)

CONTENTS

A Call to **BE**
Thriving, **H**opeful, **A**ffirming, & **T**ranscending

In the stillness before day, when everything around us is quiet, and you hear every minute move, there's a sound of possibility. It's a sound that resonates with hope for today, which turns into a personal evolution for tomorrow. These moments birth internal changes, self-reflections, the releasing of self-doubt & societal expectations, and a changed mindset.

The words in this book serve as beams of bright lights, an actionable guide that pushes you into your best self and dares you to dream beyond the present while yearning for something more. It outlines the foundation of resilience and celebrates the power that propels us into our divine destiny of purpose.

This book develops you, to be Thriving, Hopeful, Affirming, and Transcending. You can be many things, but why not choose to Be THAT! Being THAT is not a destination, but rather a journey that requires tenacity, strength, and unshakeable confidence in oneself. It is a journey that is bold, audacious, and rewarding, but only if you are fearless enough to take a step and trust that God will direct your path.

As I pen this book, I know there's a thriver in you longing to come out, I know there's hope in you ready to manifest all your dreams. I can feel the affirmer in you as your convictions come to pass, and I know there's a transcender in you ready to rise above and break down your boundaries.

As you read the following pages, you will read stories of perseverance, hope, and ambition, that are fostered through triumph and adversity. You will uncover useful tools and strategies for transforming the essence of you. Most of all, you will find that our experiences mold and shape us into the very best version of ourselves, preparing us to be better than yesterday. There's no perfection on this journey, only progress.

I invite you to join me on this daily journey, a journey where experiences turn into lessons, and life becomes a canvas designed by each of us. Our designs may be different, and our colors will vary, but even with those differences, you can still become a beautiful masterpiece, a masterpiece that gives you the Power of Be THAT and transforms the essence of you.

BE...

that!

BE that!

Your 3 Steps to **Be THAT!**

1. Psalm 46:10 – Use Psalm 46 as the Guiding Framework for Your Life!
2. Self-Reflection & Readjustment
3. Releasing Self-Doubt & Societal Expectations

BE-ing through Life's Ups and Downs

Do you know yourself? Imagine thinking that you do, only to discover that there is a new you who you've never even met!

That old you is like a stranger compared to the new you. God wants to grant you the courage and grace to simply BE this newfound person, this new you. Finding how to *Be* THAT is what this book is all about!

I used to think that the two-letter word "Be" was a simple task, an emotional state that never changed. I thought the ability to exist would come easy and simply to function could be done with little to no effort. Now, do not get me wrong, I still believe that there is a simplicity to just *Being*. However, as things change around us, we must learn how to "be" in every situation, whether those situations be positive or negative, happy or sad, comfortable or uncomfortable, certain or uncertain, confident or shy, single or married, in all the ups and downs of life.

To just be can be quite complicated. It is easy to be when everything is going as planned, when you're reaching all your goals, when you're progressing professionally, when you're in the romance of a relationship, when your kids are well behaved, when your health is top-tier, and you're living your best life. It is easy to be when you are sitting on top of the world.

What happens when your heart is burdened? How can you be when things are out of and beyond your control? When you feel like you did all the right things, only to learn you could have done them better? When you realize this is not a perfect world and people are not perfect either? When your expectations do not line up with others. What happens when life changes, and you are left to figure it all out?

I can remember trying to be after being passed over for a sought-after promotion. I can remember trying to be after working in an environment I had grown to strongly dislike. I can remember trying to be after watching my grandmother die as Alzheimer's overwhelmed her mind. I remember trying to be after going through a divorce. I can remember trying to be after experiencing heartbreak and navigating life as a single woman. I can remember trying to be after my father died in my arms at the age of 16.

I am sure you can insert your own experiences where you were trying to simply be.

Psalm 46:10 – The Guiding Framework for Your Life!

I marvel at how one could simply be in the midst of change. Change looks like chaos sometimes, but I'm convinced that there is a method to the madness. Now, if you are a woman of faith, you know that the Bible tells us in Psalm 46:10, "Be still, and know that I am God; I will be exalted among the nations, I will be exalted in the earth." (NIV) God is talking directly to us here. God is our refuge and will fight our battles for us, *all we have to do is be still.*

If you're like me, you like to fix everything immediately, but sometimes *the fixing* is simply in our ability to be still. Being still gives God the time and room to do what only He can do.

That being said, I believe that while God is fighting our battles, there is also some work we as individuals have to do.

First, we have to **self-reflect**. I am not talking about throwing a pity party for yourself, drowning in self-pity; rather, I am talking about looking at and changing ourselves instead of others. Sometimes God has to change you before He changes your situation.

Self-Reflection and Re-Adjustment

What do we do when we find ourselves in a situation we want changed?

The easy way out would be to blame everyone else, but does that serve our internal growth? Is that a healthy way to self-reflect? It is not! Blaming others is a cowardly excuse, and "excuses are tools of incompetence that build monuments of nothing."[1] We definitely do not want to build a monument of nothing!

---

[1] Henley, William E. (1875). Invictus.

Self-reflecting is Looking in a Mirror and Being Honest about What you See.

When I self reflect, I ask myself two questions:

- Who am I?
- Who do I desire to be?

I acknowledge all the things I once was, and then I call myself by the things I desire to become. To answer the second question, I look at any behaviors or actions that do not align with who I desire to become, and I release them.

This is how I set the stage for the new me!

Why do I do this? Because anytime you experience trauma or a shifting in life, it requires a new level of your being. It requires a new spirit, new dreams, elevated passion, and exponential growth, which is an increasing rate of growth over time.

This requires you to forgo the past and to move forward into the future. You are probably wondering how you move forward. You move forward by releasing. You must release self-doubt, fear, and societal expectations to embrace your authenticity.

Releasing Self Doubt and Societal Expectations

While self-doubt is not having faith in yourself, societal expectations are demands people place on you that you know nothing about. I call societal expectations the thief of authenticity. They make you feel stuck and timid, unable to move.

Societal expectations are rules that dictate what is acceptable in someone's life. They make you miserable and unfulfilled. Surely, God has more for you than that. God does not want us to live a lie to ourselves and to others. God has plans to prosper us, but He can only do that if we allow Him to alter our lives for our good. So, embrace your imperfections and use them as lessons to prepare you for your tomorrow.

Don't let imperfections cause you to have self-doubt. Your imperfections make you unique. They build character, grit, and humility. When I think about all my imperfections, I realize that I would not be who I am today without them. How could I dare to dream, to impact, to change the world if I were paralyzed by societal expectations? Metaphorically speaking, I would literally choke and die by an internal suicide, and I refuse to let unhappiness be the death of me; read that again.

I learned that societal expectations are the ignorance and limitations people place on you based on the idea of who they think you are. The truth is, people who think they know you don't and in turn have false ideas and misconceptions of who you are supposed to be. I saw a lot of this during my divorce, where people would make statements or ask questions based on their opinion, which came off as offensive and nosey.

However, the expectations of others really have nothing to do with you!

They are simply ideas of you through the lens of other people who do not know who you are or the entirety of what you have experienced. People will limit you and place you in a box. They'll place you in a box based on anything you do that goes against their expectations, that is deemed wrong and imperfect. Remember, that's their problem; not yours.

Remember to put you first, you have to rediscover your happiness and in turn rediscover who you are. What used to make you happy may no longer make you happy, and that is okay.

How do you do this?

Ask yourself questions like:

- What excites me?
- What moves me into action?
- What do I no longer have the capacity for?

You have to know what no longer serves you. This is what happens as you remove self-doubt and societal expectations.

I remember the process I had to go through to build myself up to step out on faith, start my own business, and create my own brand. It looks easy, but I went through a process to get to where I am.

I had to lose some things and had to grow into what God saw for me. I have had people ask me how do you know what God has for you, how do you know what your purpose is? As cliche as this may sound, it is true. You know God has called you to do something when you'll do it for free and still be fulfilled. You will know it is a part of your purpose when you are exhausted but can still muster up enough strength to get it done and forget you were tired in the first place.

Now do not think I'm telling you to work tired because I'm not. Rest is extremely important. I'm simply saying that sometimes your fatigue will be replaced by the mere passion you have for your purpose.

Being That: Thriving

The secret to *Be* is to readjust your being, to adjust who you are and to become who God wants you to be. Our struggle sometimes comes in when we fight against God, because we want to be one way and God has called us to be completely different. So, we find ourselves going through life experiences that are building on one another, not realizing that God is preparing us to be our best selves. We look at it as challenges and burdens, not opportunities. God looks at it as *spiritual growth*, opportunities to create intimacy between you and Him which in turn will create a better version of you.

Keep in mind that as God prepares you for better and to be better, you will have to show up with whatever God is requiring of you. Some seasons will require more prayer, more faith, more work, more determination, more love, more grace, and more transparency.

The funny thing is, you may not even think you have all these characteristics and guess what, you may not. But the God we serve has the ability to build your capacity and you do not even know it.

All seasons aren't our best seasons. Some are seasons of lessons to build our character, some are for our internal growth, some humble us and force us to reflect and figure out who we want to be, and others force us to dig deep and find something inside of us we didn't even know existed. Some seasons bring us tears, and others bring us joy.

> But regardless of the change of season,
> His grace remains the same.

What We've Learned So Far

As you reflect on your life, find comfort in the wisdom of Psalms 46:10, "Be still and know that I am God." In the spirit of self-reflection, I have found profound insights that have become the foundation of my journey. What I love about life is that our journey is indeed *our journey*, and the twists and turns truly shape us into who we are and who we become. Have you ever just sat still and allowed God to be God while reflecting on your journey?

Self-reflection has been beneficial in my quest to become better. It's in the moments of silence that I've explored the depths of my desires, dreams, passions, and been convicted to action. We do not always like to do the work that internal growth requires, but my God is it worth it!

How do you know what is inside of you if you never reflect internally? Better yet, how do you know what you need to shed, purge, or get rid of if you never assess yourself?

To truly be, you have to release the anchors of self-doubt and societal expectations while still allowing yourself to reflect. I know it is easier said than done, but you cannot let people steal your peace or weigh you down. I never understood how people could put their expectations on others anyway. I have found that many times people expect things from you they never possessed. When you reflect, reflect because you desire a better life, not because of what someone has said or because you didn't meet their expectations. Self-reflecting can be life-changing, restoring, liberating, and a celebration of a beautifully flawed essence that makes you uniquely you.

Self-reflection allows you to step into your space.

You must understand that there is space for you. I repeat, there is space for you. Whoever your inner self is calling you to be, there is a space waiting just for you, because no one can do what you can do. This space is carved out with your name on it and if you take your rightful place, there will be an abundance of blessings waiting for you to take ownership. The best characteristic of being is that there's no pressure or competition, because no one has your space or assignment.

The pursuit of simply being helps you to peel back layers of yourself and embark on a journey to unfold and discover your purpose. It's not a destination, but a continuous exploration, a revelation that aligns with your very being and existence. Releasing self-doubt and societal expectations is a courageous act of reclaiming your narrative and living in truth.

As you embrace self-reflection, discover that *vulnerability is not a weakness* but *a source of immense strength*. Fragility opens you up to growth and a space of being stretched. In the stillness of self-reflection, find the courage to challenge societal norms, to redefine success on your own terms. This may sometimes require readjustment.

Justifying Our Readjustments

To readjust is not a sign of failure, but a sign of maturity.

The changes in life require a willingness to recalibrate and to adapt. Do we really want everything to always stay the same? I am guessing no.

As time progresses, change becomes necessary. Readjusting is simply a strategy used to set you up for success when life changes around you. I can remember having to readjust at the age of 16.

There I was, the baby of the family. All my life I'd come from a two parent home and then suddenly, I found myself in a single parent home. My father had passed away suddenly and unexpectedly.

That's some readjustment for you!

I had to come to terms with the fact that my father wouldn't be at my high school or college graduation, nor would he walk me down the aisle. I would never again hear him say, "Neisha Boo," as he would so affectionately call me.

Another time I had to readjust was life after divorce.

People always want to focus on the divorce, but not on the life after divorce. What happens when you are no longer identified as a wife, when you enter those 'single streets', trying to figure who you were versus who you are becoming?

If you are like me, you ask yourself questions like, what now and who do I desire to be? It is in moments like this where you find your authentic self and start to rebuild your life. One of the things I love about God is that He will allow you to rebuild as much as you need to, and He still loves you through your journey.

It confirms that *although we can't change life, we can change ourselves.*

As you become better through being THAT, embrace Psalms 46:10 as a strong framework. Embrace your imperfections as your artistry of life, being painted with every phase you encounter. Consider it a masterpiece of your existence by self-reflecting and taking your space. Discover your purpose in the stillness God provides, and in the ever-evolving journey, be open to readjustment.

BE *that* AFFIRMATION

I will **THRIVE** no matter what yesterday was or today brings. I will have the audacity to **HOPE**, because faith is the assurance of things hoped for. I will **AFFIRM** who I am in God daily, and I will **TRANSCEND** beyond my own limitations!

JOURNAL

Welcome to the Reflective Be THAT Book Journal! Found at the end of every chapter, the journal is a space for **self-exploration and empowerment**. In these pages, you'll find prompts designed to help you delve into the concept of Be THAT and discover your inner truth.

Embrace this journey of self-reflection with openness and curiosity, knowing that each moment of introspection brings you closer to living authentically and fully.

BE *that!*

THRIVING   HOPEFUL   AFFIRMING   TRANSCENDING

CHAPTER ONE - BE

(S) (M) (T) (W) (T) (F) (S)

DATE:

Describe a recent moment when you felt fully present and engaged. What were you doing, and how did it make you feel?

List five things you're grateful for today. How do these blessings enrich your life?

Reflect on the importance of living in the present moment. How can you cultivate more presence in your daily life?

List three things that make you unique. How can you honor and celebrate these qualities.

NOTES / REMINDERS

NOTES / REMINDERS

NOTES / REMINDERS

BE...

thriving!

CHAPTER 2

BE *Thriving!*

Three Steps to Thrive:

1. Have Faith in Your Deservingness
2. Move with a Purpose & Intentionally
3. Sit in The Moments That Mean the Most

Thriving

I never really understood the word THRIVE until I became an adult. I knew what it was like to reach goals and be successful, but I had never become one with the realization of what THRIVING truly resembled, nor how it made me feel in my life. I'd heard of the word here and there during my adolescent years but didn't really know when it was actually happening, or how to truly make it happen.

I'd also heard it several times as an adult, but I'd never seen it face to face.

I can remember hearing the word thriving at conferences, professional development workshops, church services, and organizational club meetings. But it was not until I matured internally that I really understood what it meant to thrive. Up until this point, I associated the word with accomplishments and achieving goals. But what I learned on this journey of life is that for me, **thriving isn't about the successes in my life, but rather the frequency of my peace with which I can operate and function**. It is the emotion that makes me feel as if I'm aligned with my purpose, and that I can do anything I set my mind to. Thriving is the level and dimension in which I find purpose and walk in my God-given talents and gifts that allows me to be successful.

I love how God has already given us the power to Thrive.

When I reflect on thriving, I'm often reminded of **Psalm 1:3**, which compares us to *a tree planted by streams of water; that yields its fruit in season and whose leaves do not wither but prospers.*

These words are so powerful. It's a true testament that if you trust God, you will prosper. Your fruits are like your rewards, no matter how big or how small. Fruits are the positive consequences for being planted in what you believe. Can you imagine a tree by the water bearing an abundance of fruit in its proper season?

This is what happens when you thrive: whatever you touch will prosper. Let me say that again, whatever you touch will prosper, because you're so free to BE and do any and everything you desire to do. Do you believe that no matter what, you can thrive? Or that you are favored, and that God will bless every move you make in your season?

Think about how a tree's roots get nourishment from the consistency of the water, that's how we are able to thrive. The fruit has no choice but to grow because of how it's positioned and where it's positioned. Anything that is planted must grow. Just like the root of the tree draws from a steady water supply, our habits nourish our growth and the ability to flourish. Don't be afraid to plant your seeds to thrive because, ultimately, where there is nothing planted, there is no growth. Plant your seeds and be patient enough to see the fruit that in time will indeed multiply.

I remember growing up as a child we had this huge orange tree in our backyard. It was planted right in the middle of the yard by the fence. Every year our family looked forward to seeing the tree bear oranges. Some of the oranges were big, some small, and some were already bitten by the birds who would beat us to it. The oranges were the prettiest and brightest color of orange you can think of, and the juice was so sweet. My dad and I would go outside with buckets and pick every orange off the tree we could reach. We'd bring the oranges in the house and wash them off one by one. My dad would grab this beige pitcher we had and begin to squeeze each orange. He'd add a little sugar just to sweeten it up so that it was ready to drink. I remember the juice being so sweet, refreshing, replenishing, and quenching my every thirst.

This is what it feels like to thrive. It's like being replenished and becoming full. In essence, thriving is the natural outcome of being firmly rooted for the sweetness of success.

But it is easier to say the word thriving than it is to live the word thriving.

Somewhere along my journey, I lost the motivation to truly thrive. I can't say getting lost was intentional, I just think life happened and my focus and priorities weren't fixed on me, but rather, on whatever was happening around me at that time in my life. Has that ever happened to you?

Have you ever been so busy life'ing that you forget to thrive?

You forget about what that emotion felt like to pursue your dreams, or maybe you never even took the time to dream beyond your present state, because you were so caught up in your now. I have been there, and the first thing I did to change was I encouraged myself and said, "Self, you deserve to thrive, and you are capable of thriving."

Faith in your Deservingness

You have to believe that you deserve *it*!

Now I am not sure what your *it* is, but whatever it is…you most certainly deserve it. So, act like you do. Walk in it, become one with it, be steadfast in knowing that nothing can stop you but you – because you deserve it.

When you believe you deserve something, it gives you the gumption to go after whatever it is you think you deserve.

Believing you deserve something means you put yourself in places to receive whatever it is you desire. It also means you remove yourself from places and people who hinder you from who or where you thrive to be. When you believe you deserve it, there is nothing anyone can say or do to stop your momentum. Thriving allows you to be guided by this push inside of you that refuses to pursue anything other than happiness. It is a constant reminder that to grow, prosper, flourish, develop, and yes, even bloom, **you must believe that you deserve it.**

In believing that you deserve it, you give yourself permission to truly live, to let go of the limitations that you or other people placed on you, to bet on yourself and put yourself first. This is what emotional freedom looks and feels like. The ability to feel every aspect of life and still live life to its full potential without holding back.

Moving with a Purpose

You must move with a purpose and intentionality!

There needs to be a purpose behind your action. You can't just make random moves. Well, you can, but understand there are consequences to your actions. I have had a lot of moving parts in my life, but there was not always a solid intention behind it. Let's take a moment to break both words down, *move* and *intention*.

When you hear someone say *move*, of course you associate it with changing locations, positions, going from one place to another. But **to move intentionally is to move on purpose with a purpose**. It involves purposefully directing your actions in alignment with your values and goals. It's about being conscious of your choices, whether in physical movement or in life decisions. It's about ensuring that each step contributes meaningfully to your overall journey. For instance, intentionally moving through a counseling session may look like scheduling an appointment, expressing your emotions, being open to family members joining your sessions, journaling, or writing down triggers to help you heal your wounded areas.

Another example would be, instead of mindlessly scrolling through social media, decide to allocate that time to connect with family and friends more. By making a deliberate choice about how you use your time, you are actively shaping your experiences and contributing to your personal growth and well-being. In life, that means making decisions with mindful consideration; that means steering towards a destination that resonates with your deeper aspirations.

Sitting in the Meaningful Moments

As you move intentionally, it is vital to sit in the moments that mean the most.

As women, we sometimes work so hard and are so focused on the well-being of others that we forget to sit in our moments that mean the most to us. When you hear the phrase, 'sit in the moments that mean the most', you may think this has to be some grandiose achievement. However, that is not the case at all!

It simply means **taking the time to enjoy the moments that mean the most**. These are the moments you cannot get back but are cherished for a lifetime.

There are moments I wish I had sat in a bit longer… For instance, I remember my father telling me before he passed away that we were going to the jewelry store so he could purchase my birthstone ring. I was turning the sweet 16, and he wanted to do something special. It was a tradition he'd created for his family, his girls. He did the same thing with my sister, and of course he made sure I was no different.

I really did not understand the importance of sitting in that moment and appreciating everything that experience meant. It was not until I became older that I realized the magnitude of love my father showed me through that experience. I still wear the same ring to this day. I was 16 when he purchased it. At 42, the ring is just as beautiful as it was 25 years ago.

I did not sit in the meaningful moment at 16, but as an adult, I sit in that meaningful memory quite often.

Sitting in the moments that mean the most is to experience one's life consciously and fully. Instead of rushing through or overlooking important occasions, encourage yourself to be present, to reflect, to savor the value and impact of those moments.

Putting That All Together

Remember what I said about believing you deserve it? Sometimes we do not sit in our meaningful moments because we do not think we deserve it.

That's why *believing you deserve it* is the foundation for self-worth and empowerment. It sets the stage for pursuing your goals with confidence, recognizing that your aspirations are valid and that you are worthy. *Moving intentionally* complements this by emphasizing purposeful actions aligned with your beliefs and goals. It transforms aspirations into tangible steps, ensuring that every move contributes meaningfully to your journey. *Sitting in moments that mean the most* completes the cycle, allowing you to relish and enjoy your experiences. This practice instills gratitude and mindfulness, fostering a deeper appreciation for the milestones you've reached and the growth you've experienced.

> These elements together create a powerful synergy for personal fulfillment to thrive.

The truth is, what thriving looks like for you may be different than what thriving looks like to others. What is success? can be different depending on who you ask, so can thriving. So, what is *thriving* to me?

Thriving is growing!

It is something that never truly ends and is triggered by action. It's triggered by believing you deserve it, moving intentionally, and sitting in the moments that mean the most. Take some time to believe you deserve it, move with purpose and intentionally, and sit in the moments that mean the most, because this will create in you a heart of gratitude.

How do we thrive?

Guess what? You already know! I just gave you the three steps!

Thriving begins with a foundational belief in your **deservingness of success**—a mindset that empowers you to pursue goals confidently. **Moving intentionally** involves purposeful actions and decisions, navigating life with a clear direction rather than drifting aimlessly. Additionally, **sitting in moments that mean the most** emphasizes the importance of mindfulness, savoring and appreciating the significant experiences that contribute to a fulfilling life. Combining these elements fosters a holistic approach to thriving, and no one thrives the way you do, we all thrive in our own individuality.

So, what's next?

In order for you to thrive, you have to *define it for yourself.* What does it mean to you? Is thriving overcoming your challenges and making your own personalized mark in the world? Are you content with not truly living and just breathing? In my 42 years of living, I have realized that we rise by lifting others and giving them the capacity to be, learn, and grow. Thriving is about feeling your best and attracting the things that are assigned to you and then operating in that assignment.

Moreover, thriving is not a destination; it's a continuous journey of self-discovery and growth. Life is not for us to fear the U-turns, but to embrace them as opportunities for evolution. The beauty of life lies in its unpredictability, and therein lies the potential for unparalleled growth. There have been times when I was afraid to grow because there were people I was afraid to lose. I knew that growing would require me to detach from people I was not ready to detach from. However, I did it because it was vital to the journey God has set for me. It was vital because that is what it takes to thrive.

Do you have the courage to thrive, to let go of what's familiar and encounter the unknown?

Thriving has allowed me to embark on an internal exploration I'd never known otherwise. Thriving has given me the ability to not only push myself, but to push others. I have found I'm most filled with thriving when I'm around others who thrive as well. My be That energy is contagious and can push someone beyond their wildest dream.

As you begin and continue to thrive, repeat these words:

BE *that!* AFFIRMATION

I will **THRIVE** no matter what yesterday was or today brings. I will have the audacity to **HOPE**, because faith is the assurance of things hoped for. I will **AFFIRM** who I am in God daily, and I will **TRANSCEND** beyond my own limitations!

CHAPTER ONE - BE THRIVING   (S) (M) (T) (W) (T) (F) (S)

DATE:

Set specific goals and aspirations related to thriving. What steps can you take to further cultivate a sense of thriving in your life? How do you envision your life evolving as you continue to prioritize your well-being?

Take a moment to express gratitude for the things in your life that contribute to your sense of thriving. This could include supportive relationships, personal achievements, opportunities for growth, etc. How does practicing gratitude enhance your overall well-being?

Reflect on any challenges or obstacles you are facing that may be hindering your ability to thrive. How do these challenges affect your overall sense of well-being? What strategies can you use to overcome these obstacles?

Describe any self-care practices you have been engaging in to promote your well-being. How do these practices contribute to your ability to thrive? Are there any additional self-care strategies you would like to explore?

NOTES / REMINDERS

NOTES / REMINDERS

NOTES / REMINDERS

BE...

hopeful!

CHAPTER 3

BE *hopeful!*

Three Steps to Hope:

1. Communicate in a Language of Faith-Talk
2. Practice Resilience & Boldness
3. Wake Up in Expectation

Hope

There have been so many times where I found myself thirsty for hope.

Whether it was for something I desired to happen in the future, or for the present, I longed for the glimmer of light guided by the force of hope. Hope shows itself at the intersection of change. It is a guiding light that empowers us as individuals to rise above challenges and seize opportunities.

Hope gives us the audacity to engage in Faith Talk, to be bold, and to wake up every day in expectation. Hope outlines our faith. And faith paints a picture of what you can't see yet.

Faith is rooted deep. It's real and strong. Some days, it's uncertain and other days it's strong as than hell. Even if it's weak, our faith must never fade. I've had so many moments where faith saved me not because things were perfect, but because I was covered and protected by my faith. If you can have faith outlined in hope, there is no doubt that you can Faith Talk, be bold, and wake up in expectation.

I often say, 'Never allow dimmed hope to cause you to lose hope, because anywhere where it seems dim has an opportunity for light.'

We should find hope in every minute, hour, and day that we are blessed to experience. That includes the hard times. There have been times my eyes were filled with tears, times I felt like I was carrying the world on my back, times when I was not sure which way to go and which way to turn, times when embarrassment seemed unbearable, and life was colored with uncertainty. I found hope in those moments too.

How do we find hope in our adverse circumstances?

Whenever I find my hope diminishing, I lend myself to **Hebrews 11:1** which says that "Faith is the foundation in which things are hoped for and proof of things unseen."

If you're breathing, I'm sure at some point in your life you've been introduced to hope. When I think of hope, faith immediately follows. I've come to believe you can't have one without the other. I think of hope and faith like a math equation. Just like 2+2 equals 4, faith + hope equals the solution to so many things we face. I like to think of hope as a light that guides us and provides the extra push that we need to reach things that seem distant or unreachable. Hope combined with faith creates a dynamic synergy that we as humans yearn for to be brilliant in the midst of what life may bring us.

There's something about having the foundation of hope that gives assurance. It brings comfort to hidden forces that move us into action. The Hebrews verse emphasizes the emotion of believing and shaping our outlooks and guiding our actions. It proposes that faith warrants us to imagine outcomes beyond what we see. Don't let what you see make you forget what God has already said. Be courageous and persistent so you can be fulfilled and live in your divine purpose. Be confident in all the possibilities and stand on your unwavering faith and hope.

Sometimes hope doesn't just involve you, but it also involves others. Having my own business and being an educator gives me a unique advantage over the various arenas where one can impart and find hope. As an educator, I rely on hope daily. I leave my house and head to a school campus where my goal is to positively impact the lives of over one thousand students. Some students come from high, middle, and low socioeconomic status families, but they all still require hope. Hope in their future is what keeps me motivated to push them. It's the look in their eyes when they need a hug, support, or praise and attention. The same hope you should see in yourself, you should see in others. Hope doesn't see color, age, circumstance or background; it only sees the betterment of others and the essence of you.

Hope is not always easy.

I can remember one experience as if it happened just yesterday. It was a hot day in March, and I was home after going to a doctor's appointment for a condition called Bell's Palsy. I'll explain what that is later in the chapter. My father was home recovering from prostate cancer surgery. My mother had gone out to run errands after dropping me off. The phone rang and it was for my dad.

I left my room to bring him the telephone and to, my life-changing surprise, there was my father on the ground and unresponsive.

I immediately went into a panic. I screamed and cried. I called 911, and they began to walk me through the steps for mouth-to-mouth resuscitation. I remember placing my dad's head on my lap and putting my mouth to his as I tried to put life back into him. I could feel him take his last breath in my arms as tears rolled down my face.

It was at this moment that I knew hope like never before.

I could feel it, and at some point, I became one with it. Hope filled all my being. The gift of hope is so strong that even after my dad took his last breath, I still hold onto hope today.

How Hope becomes Faith-Talk

Hope has taught me that Faith-Talk is essential to my well-being. So, what is Faith-Talk? I'm glad you asked!

Faith-Talk is **the ability to positively talk yourself through something**. Every time I use Faith-Talk, I make sure I include God. That's because Faith-Talk is a conversation, a conversation centered around faith, that dives into the profound belief in Someone beyond the tangible.

Faith-Talk emphasizes the role of faith in navigating life's uncertainties and challenges. Faith-Talk has gotten me through some of the toughest and most exciting times in my life. It's the act of talking yourself out of negativity, fear, and doubt.

If you desire to use Faith-Talk, there is one thing you're going to need to do.

You need to surround yourself with some faith talkers so they can motivate and inspire you!

If you are constantly around naysayers and people who don't believe in you, you won't believe in yourself. But get in the company of people who believe God is their source, get around people who know their purpose is larger than themselves, and get around people who don't think believing in you will take attention from them. In addition, **remind yourself who you are and *whose* you are**. You are God's! You have the authority over the negative noises that try to sneak into your head. You have the authority to have faith talk. So how do we demonstrate Faith Talk?

Practicing Faith-Talk

Let's practice. Say these words with me:

- "God said that I am the head and not the tail."
- "God said He wishes for me to prosper."
- "God said I can do all things."
- "God said if my hope is in Him, He will renew my strength."
- "God said I am more than a conquerer."
- "God said no weapons formed against me shall prosper."

Now I could say all these things without including God, but they would be empty phrases without Him. Whereas including Him activates these words and our faith. It lets God know you're tapping into and standing on the power of His word. You may have your own style of Faith-Talk; there is no specific way to do this, but however you talk, be sure that you are encouraging yourself through your faith.

> However you choose to Faith-Talk, make sure
> it encourages, uplifts, and motivates you.

Faith-Talk Builds Resilience

There have been several times when I had to use Faith-Talk to get me through a crisis, but one experience that comes to mind is when I was diagnosed with Bell's Palsy.

John Hopkins Medicine defines Bell's Palsy as, "an unexplained episode of facial muscle weakness or paralysis. This condition results from damage to the facial nerve. It causes pain and discomfort and usually occurs on one side of the face or head."

I remember my facial muscles being extremely weak, and one side of my face would droop. My smile was crooked, and it looked like I'd had a stroke. I would have headaches, loss of ability to taste, and had to sleep with an eye patch, because the eye on the side affected would not close. My entire side was weak including my arms, legs, everything. I have had Bell's Palsy manifest itself twice, once on both sides of my face.

So, when you see me smiling just know there's a story behind my smile.

This experience made me Faith-Talk like never before. God heard my words and restored me, but I had to believe in what I couldn't see. That's how Faith-Talk builds resilience. What does it mean to be resilient?

Resilience is the ability to bounce back from setbacks. Resilience is the core of hope. Research indicates that individuals with a hopeful outlook are more adept at coping with stressors, exhibiting a greater capacity to adapt and thrive in the face of adversity. By cultivating hope, we fortify our mental defenses, creating a shield against the storms that life inevitably throws our way.

In other words, resilience is a mechanism for mental wellness. It allows us to confront challenges with a constructive attitude. Embracing hope empowers us to reframe difficulties as opportunities for growth, reducing the psychological toll of stressors. I know stress is something we can all relate to.

In finding my own individuality, life has taught me how to be resilient. I'm convinced that in order to hope, resilience is a trait you must possess. You must be resilient to hope, because resilience gives you the will to bounce back from adversity and challenges. There is no way you can grow, reach new heights, or become successful, without having the characteristic of resilience.

Resilience allows you to become a version of yourself you've never been before because every experience, positive or negative, contributes to who you are or who you're becoming. In other words, you can't grow without going through something, and every time you have a different experience, it deepens and grows your resilience. Your resilience at 25 is different from your resilience at 35. And your resilience at 35 is different from your resilience at 45. Your resilience at 45 is different from your resilience at 55. Why? Because the more knowledge we gain from the experiences we encounter, the more we can apply the lessons we've learned and add a new depth to our resilience.

Advantages of Resilience

There are advantages to being resilient. These advantages include being able to adapt to change, to cope with setbacks, to have enhanced problem-solving skills, to have an emotional well-being, to be able to self-discover, to have a positive mindset, to build stronger relationships, to have personal empowerment, and to have long-term growth and development. These advantages not only help you thrive, but they allow you to function while still navigating through life. Let's explore each advantage.

Adapting to Change

This means you can navigate through uncertainties and challenges. This doesn't mean change will be easy, but you will have the capacity to manage the challenges.

Coping with Setbacks

This will allow you to bounce back from disappointments and overcome failures, which builds character.

Problem Solving

This provides you with a different point of view. It allows you to view obstacles as challenges to be addressed rather than running from the situation.

Emotional Well-Being

Emotional well-being gives you the ability to manage stress and anxiety and have a more balanced emotional state.

Self-Discovery

This allows you to understand yourself better and learn from experiences. This is where the opportunity is for God to mold you and shape you into what you are destined to be.

Confidence

Confidence is using the success you've had through other challenges to assist you in future challenges.

Positive Mindset

Having a positive mindset means being optimistic with positive thoughts. This doesn't mean you don't have negative thoughts; this just means you don't allow your negative thoughts to overshadow your positive thoughts.

Building Stronger Relationships

This allows you to positively influence your interactions with others and foster stronger social connections. This is important as social connections are what help us thrive as individuals.

Personal Empowerment

This empowers you to take control of your life! It encourages proactive decision-making and goal-setting.

Long Term Growth & Development

Last but certainly not least, long-term growth and development is an ongoing personal growth that ensures a continuous process of development throughout your life.

Incorporate resilience into your life today, and these 10 advantages will manifest in you!

Boldness

Once you have mastered Faith Talk, you can now be bold. What does it mean to be bold? Being bold means **to be fearless, daring, and willing to take risks**. It is stepping out on faith not knowing how things will turn out but doing it anyway. I like to compare being bold to someone who stands out in a crowd not because of the noise they make, but because of the impact they have made and the change they bring.

If you think about history, some of the most well-known people have been people who were bold.

Whether you like them or not, they take risks and do not let what other people are doing get in their way or distract them. When I think about people who are bold, Beyonce is one of the first people that comes to mind, not because of the records she has sold, but because of her work ethic and action to be the best in her craft. She is willing to do what others are not. She is intentional about her art and knows how to be unique without jeopardizing her authenticity. What are you willing to do that others are not willing to do?

That is what makes you bold, and that is what elevates you from being mediocre to operating in excellence.

One of the things I love about being bold is it defies conformity. Defying conformity is a refusal to be confined by societal expectations or predefined roles. Another thing I love about being bold is the courageous self-expression it lends to an individual. At the heart of boldness lies the courage to express oneself authentically no matter who it makes feel uncomfortable. From societal norms to personal insecurities, there are countless forces that attempt to stifle our voices. I'm amazed at how the power of bold self-expression sets you apart from others.

Being bold requires you to not worry about what others say but to have your own control knowing that whatever God is asking you to do, you do it.

As I reflect on being bold, I think about the amount of courage it took to create be That. When God originally gave me the vision, I said to myself, what would allow me to have an impact, touch my community and the world? How would little ole me be received and/or respected for something I had never done before?

You have no idea the boldness it took for me to walk in my purpose, how every time I thought I was ready, there was a voice saying, 'No, you are not.'

So, guess what I did? I did it anyway!

In the words of Lauren Hill, 'Ready or not, here I come!' That is exactly what I did. I am not where I want to be yet, but thank God I was bold enough to get started. I sometimes still hear that voice saying, 'You are not ready' or 'Your idea will not work'; the only difference now is that my bold Faith-Talk is much louder than the voice that says I can't.

Boldness & Waking Up in Expectation

Allowing Faith-Talk to dominate my mind helps me to wake up in expectation.

If you use your faith to wake up in expectation daily, there is no reason why you shouldn't be bold. Anything negative that enters your mind should be cast out by your faith. This allows you to operate in expectation and be bold because you know that you have prepared and are ready to step out on faith and do something that you have been longing to do.

Does this mean you will not be scared? Nope! Does this mean that you will not doubt yourself? Nope! But what it does mean is that in spite of all this, you'll do it anyway. That is what will move you into being bold.

> Some people say walk in expectation,
> I say wake up in expectation.

This means that as soon as you open your eyes, expect new blessings, miracles, favor, and everything that is good and perfect. Expect doors to open that you didn't see coming, expect to meet people who can help you achieve your dreams and check off all your goals. Even when you hear something that disappoints or saddens you, expect God to turn it around in your favor. If you wake up in expectation, your attitude will be different, and your spirit will shine, so that others see the expectation in you.

There are days where I can literally feel the blessings on the way, that's how connected you are when waking up in expectation.

It's not a matter of if it will happen, but a matter of when it will happen. My question to you is, do you wake up in expectation? And if you do, are you ready for your prayers to be answered?

As someone who pours into others, I never know where my next speaking engagement or business opportunity will come from, but I expect opportunities to fall fresh on me. If I am honest, more than half of the things I do I never see coming, but God keeps providing. You know why? Because I expect it!

I'm telling you this not to brag, because that's never been my style, I'm telling you this so you know that you don't have to always have everything perfect.

Don't let perfection cause you to procrastinate and miss what God has for you. Wake up in expectation and trust that it's going to happen.

Waking up in expectation is more than just a routine; it's a conscious decision to embrace the day with optimism and anticipation. My mornings serve as a sacred space for setting the tone of my daily narrative. Waking up in expectation is an intentional act, a declaration that today holds possibilities waiting to unfold. It's about cultivating a mindset that anticipates growth, resilience, and moments of joy.

What do you do to set the tone and mood for your day? How do you start your mornings so that your day is productive and meaningful? I have found that waking up in expectation can change the trajectory of not only my day, but my entire life.

AS YOU CONTINUE TO HOPE, REPEAT YOUR

BE *that!* AFFIRMATION

I will **THRIVE** no matter what yesterday was or today brings. I will have the audacity to **HOPE** because faith is the assurance of things hoped for. I will **AFFIRM** who I am in God daily and I will **TRANSCEND** beyond my own limitations!

CHAPTER ONE - BE HOPEFUL   (S) (M) (T) (W) (T) (F) (S)

DATE:

Reflect on your current state of mind regarding hopefulness. How do you feel about your future prospects and the possibilities that lie ahead? Describe any recent experiences, observations or people that give you hope.

Based on your previous response, reflect on how these sources of hope contribute to your overall well-being.

Reflect on any challenges you are facing. How do these challenges affect your sense of hopefulness? Discuss instances where you have demonstrated resilience in the face of adversity and how these experiences have shaped your outlook on hope.

Consider the role of mindset in cultivating hope. How do your beliefs and attitudes influence your ability to remain hopeful in difficult times? Reflect on any shifts in perspective that have helped you maintain a sense of hope.

NOTES / REMINDERS

NOTES / REMINDERS

NOTES / REMINDERS

BE...

affirming!

BE *affirming!*

Three Steps to Affirm:

1. Cultivate a Changed Mindset
2. Incorporate Repetition in Your Daily Routine
3. Believe who God says You Are

Affirming

If you research the word affirm, you will find that it means, 'to positively state and declare something that is said, believed or something you are able to do'. Affirming is having the ability to know that something can happen for you if you just believe that it will. Affirming exudes confidence and reassures that the practice of continuously believing something will eventually turn into what you have affirmed to be true. It's like a fire that burns so deeply that even when the flames can no longer be seen, the heat continues to stir within you, causing you to affirm what you truly desire.

Affirming is probably something you've done before whether you were aware of it or not. We all affirm! Maybe you've had thoughts over and over about the same thing, hoping that it turned out in your favor. Or maybe you were waiting to hear some news hoping it was good news. You may have kept thinking and telling yourself, things are going to be fine, it's going to turn out the way it should, and it's working out for my good.

Affirming is emotionally supporting an idea or belief.

Affirming is like having an instinct or burst of positivity. Anytime my affirmations fall short, or I get an affirmation block, I just allow those instincts to kick back in with the help of **Philippians 4:8**. These influential words express that *whatever is true, noble, right, pure, lovely, admirable, excellent and praiseworthy are things we should constantly think about.* It means we should acknowledge and reinforce positive thoughts and qualities so much to the point of even verbalizing it at times.

Drowning out negativity is a must when affirming. You can't see or recognize your light when you're consumed by darkness, dark thoughts, dark words, or dark deeds. Don't get lost in the shadows of negativity, but rather speak with conviction of who you are and who you aspire to be. Operating in negativity holds us back sometimes. Have you ever wondered why the things you desire aren't happening?

Perhaps it's because you have failed to speak it into existence. Now don't think just because you say something it's going to happen. Affirmation only works when you put in the work! It serves as the engine that drives your destiny. You can't operate without fuel; you have to put something into it to get something out of it. And you can't just put anything into yourself either.

Think about what happens when you put the wrong grade of gas in your car tank. It could cause your car to not function correctly and could even damage various parts of your engine. The same thing goes for you, if you don't pour what's considered to be the best grade into yourself, you won't see the best results.

I challenge you to affirm like nobody's business, like your life depends on it, and honestly, it does. Well, at least your quality of life does. The more you see for yourself, the more you can accomplish. Imagine affirming something in your life and boom, with prayer and hard work, it happens. Can you imagine that feeling? Believe in yourself, begin to affirm, and watch how it changes your life. With dedication and faith, your affirmations can turn into answered prayers. Be mindful that consistency is key; keep affirming, and God will make your affirmations real life testimonies.

Cultivating a Changed Mindset

One of the things that you must take into consideration is that to truly affirm, you must believe it. In order to do this, you have to change your mindset. You have to have a growth mindset. A fixed mindset may cause us to shy away from challenges because we do not want to feel embarrassed. We are afraid to make mistakes, and in turn we avoid challenges that we could overcome and grow from.

When we embrace a growth mindset, we can view challenges not as insurmountable obstacles, but as opportunities to enhance our skills and learn. The willingness and ability to have a growth mindset requires you to be intentional and consistent. It literally forces you to allow your positive thoughts to overtake your negative thoughts and operate in positivity rather than negativity. It requires a new way of thinking to become the very best version of who you desire to be.

Don't get me wrong, having a growth mindset is not always easy, because it puts you in uncomfortable positions. But how do you progress and grow if you're always comfortable? Where is the change and development in that? There really is none.

Here are the steps to affirm and grow in your mindset:

- Be willing to identify your goals (create goals you want to achieve)
- Use positive language (focus on what you want to achieve by using empowering words)
- Be present and specific (use statements that reflect your current reality or the reality you are actively creating)
- Keep it personal (make sure it's your personal experiences)
- Make it believable (make sure you can realistically do it)
- Engage your senses (visualize and feel the outcomes of your affirmations)
- Combine this with actions (take steps toward your goals and align your behavior with the positive statements you're making)
- Write your goals with a timeline (journal to revisit and stay on track)
- Adapt as needed (be flexible to make changes)
- Repeat regularly (repeat these steps as often as possible)

These steps are necessary to embrace a mindset that will move you forward!

Incorporate Repetition in Your Daily Routine

Repetition is simply saying the same thing over and over. That is exactly what you must do when you are affirming things in your life. The key to affirming is being consistent. Repeat your affirmations regularly and include them in your life daily. Repetition reinforces the positive messages in your mind in hope of results.

Repetition enhances the effectiveness of affirmations. Repetition provides a subconscious influence, builds confidence, and cultivates habits. If we look at the subconscious influence; we learn that the more we repeat something, the more our mind believes it to be true. This will then begin to influence your behaviors and beliefs.

Repetition plays a significant role in shaping thoughts, behaviors, and habits. The idea behind repetition is that consistent and repeated actions or thoughts can lead to changes that last. As a little girl, my mother would make me repeat the spelling of my middle name over and over. I remember thinking it was so hard to spell. Mom and I would sit down at the table and begin to repeat Monyette until I mastered how to spell and say my middle name. It was the practice of repetition that made the correct spelling and pronunciation stay stuck in my mind.

This is why repetition is important when affirming. Repetition cultivates how our behaviors are rooted and strengthens the connection between our stimuli and responses. When affirming, repetition is often employed to establish positive habits and thought patterns. For example, sometimes I use written affirmations of repetition to incorporate in my daily routine. I know that everyday I'm going to look in the mirror before I walk out the door for work. So, I take the red lipstick and write the things I want God to manifest in my life. This is inclusive of goals and even what I believe and think about myself. As I look at the mirror, I'm reminded of every word I write and what it takes for each thing listed to come to pass.

We have to be careful because **repetition works with positive and negative behaviors**, so it is vital to watch what we do and say, because sometimes a negative habit forms before we know it. This could be destructive behaviors or dwelling on negative thoughts, which can reinforce detrimental patterns. Being mindful of the nature of our repetition is critical to our power for personal development.

Building self-confidence is also vital when incorporating repetition. It impacts your abilities and the determination you have to achieve a task. This increases your confidence and translates it into positive actions and outcomes.

I Am Defined by Who God Says I Am

The act of regularly affirming positive statements becomes part of your routine, reinforcing the positive messages consistently. This brings me to the good part: Believing who God says you are!

Sometimes we get so caught up in today's hustle and bustle that we forget who we are in God. It amazes me how we let what others say dictate our mood swings, behaviors, and emotions when really, **nothing matters except what God has said**. I'm guilty of this too. And so, whenever I find myself worried about other people and what they said or did, I try to hear from God. Hearing from God gives me direction as to how to proceed. Life takes us through experiences that show God to be God. So, the question then becomes, who does God say you are?

I know you've heard what others say about you,
but what does God say?

If you are a believer, you know that God says you are:

1. A New Creation in Christ

"Therefore, if anyone is in Christ, he is a new creation; the old has passed away, and see, the new has come!" (2 Cor. 5:17)

2. A Child of God

"But to all who did receive him, he gave them the right to be children of God, to those who believe in his name" (John 1:12).

3. A Branch of the True Vine

"I am the vine; you are the branches. The one who remains in me and I in him produces much fruit, because you can do nothing without me" (John 15:5).

4. Justified and Redeemed

"They are justified freely by his grace through the redemption that is in Christ Jesus" (Rom. 3:24).

5. An Heir

"We are God's children, and if children, also heirs—heirs of God and coheirs with Christ—if indeed we suffer with him so that we may also be glorified with him" (Rom. 8:17).

6. A Temple of the Holy Spirit

"Don't you know that your body is a temple of the Holy Spirit who is in you, whom you have from God? You are not your own" (1 Cor. 6:19)

7. A Member of Christ's Body

"Now you are the body of Christ, and individual members of it" (1 Cor. 12:27).

8. An Ambassador for Christ

"Therefore, we are ambassadors for Christ, since God is making his appeal through us. We plead on Christ's behalf: 'Be reconciled to God'" (2 Cor. 5:20)

9. Chosen

"For he chose us in him, before the foundation of the world, to be holy and blameless in love before him" (Eph. 1:4)

10. Redeemed and Forgiven

"In him we have redemption through his blood, the forgiveness of our trespasses, according to the riches of his grace" (Eph. 1:7).

11. God's Workmanship

"For we are his workmanship, created in Christ Jesus for good works, which God prepared ahead of time for us to do" (Eph. 2:10)

12. No longer a Slave, but Free

"For freedom, Christ set us free. Stand firm then and don't submit again to a yoke of slavery" (Gal. 5:1).

These are just *some* of the scriptures that resonate with me, but there are so many more. Take the time to research and see what scriptures resonate with you. At times, when you forget or need a reminder of who God says you are, read these words and know that regardless of what other people may say, **what God says is the real prize.**

One of the things I love about God is that even when we don't think we are qualified or who we should be in Him, He still qualifies us. My prayer is that we can see ourselves as God sees us. The more we see ourselves the way God sees us, the more we can operate *in purpose and on purpose*, because we have nothing holding us back. Think about all the things that you could've done by now at this point in your life, but something held you back. That something kept you from writing that book, going back to school, starting that business, and going for the promotion. How much of your future have you delayed by not even going after your dreams? What do those blessings look like that God still has waiting on you? I dare you to go back in your mind and think about all the aspirations you once had and how you can bring them to life.

> ### The world needs you and the light that your dreams bring.

I remember God whispering to me about starting Be THAT. I remember saying, God, no one is going to listen to me because they don't know me, this is a new space for me, I'm divorced and far from perfect. God answered back and said, that's why I want to use you, because you are all of those things.

Bringing it all Together

A couple years back, I was the speaker at a women's conference. I'd compiled all my thoughts to present to these women of God, and I remember getting to a certain point in my notes where I began to speak from my heart. No notes, just pure authenticity. I talked about my divorce, starting life over as a single woman, and how every day is an opportunity to be better than before.

The response from these women brought tears to my eyes.

There were so many women who could relate to my story, to my tears, to my struggles, but most of all, to the fact that God had restored me and was using me as His vessel for the women in that room. That is when I knew that my purpose was real, and that God's whispers were evident in my life. There are some things evident in your life too, but you've first got to believe that you are who God says you are. In order to really internalize that you are who God says you are, you must experience a changed mindset. I mentioned this earlier in the chapter but let's go a little deeper.

A changed mindset is the way in which we view the world. It is the act of changing your mental attitude, beliefs, and perspectives. This mindset recognizes that change is a constant in life and embraces it as an opportunity for growth and improvement. It often involves challenging existing thought patterns, questioning assumptions, and being open to new ideas. Many times, this is difficult to do, especially when you have been raised a certain way. Sometimes it's like erasing everything you've learned and replacing it with an entirely new belief system. I often think that when traumatic experiences happen to us, it opens up space to create a changed mindset.

Life has a tendency to make us rethink and reevaluate how we function. How you think has a high impact on what you do.

A key aspect of a changed mindset is the recognition that personal development and progress requires a willingness to step out of your comfort zone. It involves overcoming fear of the unknown and embracing challenges as opportunities to learn. A changed mindset is characterized by adaptability, resilience, and a positive outlook toward change. The backbone to having a changed mindset is knowing and believing that what you believe is aligned with who you are and who you're becoming.

Developing a changed mindset may involve setting realistic goals, breaking them down into manageable steps, and celebrating small victories along the way. It also requires cultivating a sense of curiosity and a willingness to learn from experiences, whether positive or negative. One of the benefits of a changed mindset is that you can have a changed mindset at any time. You can change your mind whenever you see fit, just be consistent and stand on what you truly believe.

As you grow in affirmation, it is a perfect time to implement what I call the Personal Growth Factor into your life. I have found that when you are intentional about affirming who you are, and you genuinely want to become better, having a guide or reference helps to keep you on track to meet your desired goal.

The Personal Growth Factor is a great way to remind yourself how to tap into your affirmation and your ability to grow personally:

P - Perseverance

Affirmation pivots you into perseverance. It is a driving force that pushes you through difficulties and fuels your growth.

G - Growth Mindset

Cultivate a growth mindset by embracing affirmations as a strategy through challenges and opportunities to learn and develop.

R - Resilience

Resilience is the cornerstone of personal growth and affirming who you are.

O - Optimism

Maintain optimism in challenging situations. Affirm that things will work out in your favor.

W - Wisdom from Experiences

Extract wisdom from life experiences and include those experiences to enhance your affirmations.

T - Transformation

Personal growth involves transformation which cannot be done without having a positive perspective and outlook on life. You must believe the transformation is possible.

H - Harnessing Strengths

Identify and harness your strengths. Who you tell yourself you are will determine who you become.

AS YOU CONTINUE TO BE AFFIRMING,
PLEASE REPEAT THE FOLLOWING
WORDS FROM YOUR

BE *that!* AFFIRMATION

I will **THRIVE** no matter what yesterday was or what today brings. I will have the audacity to **HOPE** because faith is the assurance of things hoped for. I will **AFFIRM** who I am in God daily and I will **TRANSCEND** beyond my own limitations!

CHAPTER FOUR - BE AFFIRMING   Ⓢ Ⓜ Ⓣ Ⓦ Ⓣ Ⓕ Ⓢ

DATE:

Reflect on your current state of mind regarding affirmation. How do you feel about yourself and your abilities? Describe any recent experiences or observations that have influenced your sense of self-affirmation.

Reflect on any practices you engage in to affirm yourself. This could include positive affirmations, visualization exercises, self-care routines, etc. How do these practices help you cultivate a positive self-image and mindset?

Reflect on the importance of setting boundaries as a form of self-affirmation. How do you prioritize your needs and well-being in your relationships and interactions with others? What boundaries do you need to establish or reinforce to affirm yourself?

Take a moment to engage in positive self-reflection. What are some qualities or strengths that you appreciate about yourself? How do these attributes contribute to your overall well-being and sense of self-worth?

NOTES / REMINDERS

NOTES / REMINDERS

NOTES / REMINDERS

BE...

transcending!

BE *Transcending!*

Three Steps to Transcend:

1. Listen to God's "Yes" and "No"
2. Surround Yourself with People who are Limitless & Supportive
3. Maintain Consistency & Visualize Success

Transcenders

When I think about the people I've been influenced by, I think about people who go beyond ordinary limits, who reach a level that is unexpected and unusual. These are the people who transcend and are known as *transcenders*.

I'm sure you know someone who is a transcender, someone who did their part or is currently doing their part to change the world and to impact communities, someone who brings people together, who, in spite of different cultures or beliefs, can still view people as humans and bring that compassion to the work they offer up. Transcenders help others become better by rendering their services and offering their gifts towards a much bigger cause. Transcenders take their gifts and, because of the authority their gifts carry, can do things that aren't seen every day.

Some may even say transcenders are uncommon. Transcenders are different. People tend to want to mimic transcenders without understanding their purpose, their anointing, and their journey.

I personally believe that there's a transcender in all of us.

Yes, that means that there is a transcender in you too!

So the question becomes, who does God say you are and do you believe Him?

Listening to God's Yes and No

The first thing you have to do to transcend is to listen to God's yes and no. I know it sounds deep, but I promise you, if you seek God and develop an intimate relationship with Him, you'll hear His voice at the most pivotal times. If for some reason you don't hear His voice, keep listening. For me, His voice is that spiritual voice that guides and directs me.

If you are a believer, you have that spiritual power too, you just have to tap into it and be aware. You have to be listening. It's important to keep in mind that God speaking to us doesn't always sound the same. Sometimes God speaks to us through other people, through experiences, or through signs and wonders. When we are able to connect with God, He can give us direction in using these things.

I'm always moved at how God will whisper a yes or no as we journey through life. I remember contemplating whether I would go back to school to finish my doctorate degree and God nudged my spirit with a yes and said, 'If you go back to school, I will help you complete your degree.'

Or the time when I couldn't understand why certain relationships ended beyond my control, that was God's, 'No.'

Or even the time I thought a certain partnership wouldn't work because of different variables and God politely said, 'Yes, it will.'

Listening to God's yes and no isn't always easy, especially when it takes you out of your comfort zone. God's no can take you out one circle and place you in another circle because your circle doesn't fit your goals. God's no can keep you in a place you are tired of being in, but you must remain there when God says it's not time to move yet. God's yeses and noes are not always what we want to hear, but we have to remember that **all things work together for our good, even the things we may not understand.**

I always remind myself that just because it's a yes or no right now doesn't mean it will always be a yes or no. This is why it is important to stay connected to God, so you can know when and if His answer changes.

Surround Yourself with People who are Limitless & Supportive

In order to be a transcender, you have to surround yourself with people who are limitless. These are the people who always strive for greatness. They are always thinking of how to be better and how to do more. If they do something one time, just know that when they do it again, it will be bigger and better.

Limitless people are driven by excellence. They challenge themselves for new possibilities and are on a continuous journey to be the best in what they do. Limitless individuals refuse to be confined to a box. They are always thinking creatively and non-traditionally because they don't put limits on themselves.

Think about all the people who you would categorize as a transcender. At some point in their lives, they took the brakes off and pressed go. I'm sure they encountered disappointment, failure, and various challenges, but they kept going anyway, because they were determined to not be stopped, and determined to function on their own terms. This is what you have to do to be a transcender: Surround yourself with transcenders and people who are limitless and want to see you win.

Transcenders are the people who love you and want to see you win. They are not jealous or envious. As a matter of fact, they may believe in you more than you believe in yourself. Supportive people motivate you when you want to give up and pray for you when your spirit is down. They remind you that you can start again, start over, and still achieve greatness. Surround yourself with people who uplift you and celebrate your victories, people who will give you the advice you can trust and unwavering love.

> **Transcending doesn't just happen, you have to be intentional about being a transcender.**

Remember, who you surround yourself with is a huge part of that, because we become who we hang around, or at least are influenced by them.

Maintain Consistency

Something else that has worked for me and transcenders alike is to be consistent. Consistency is doing something over and over again. Consistency is a behavior that you commit to which can produce certain outcomes. If I say I'm a business owner who specializes in mentorship, motivational speaking, facilitating workshops and providing educational tools, then everything I do in my business should be centered around those things. My posts, collaborations, videos and so forth, should always go back to the services I offer and the mission and vision of the business.

This is how you build trust and gain and keep clients. People have to know that if they do business with you, you are committed to the end product.

Consistency shows people the range of your talents. When you are consistent, people can see who you truly are, and sometimes they see things in you that you didn't even know were there. My consistency has opened up so many opportunities for me and continues to do so. People know who I am and what I offer, and I have the receipts to back it up. There is fruit as a result of your consistency, whether it comes through impact, financial gain, or lifelong connections.

You will see the results of your consistency.

Visualize Success

After you've built your consistency in your purpose, you now have to visualize your success.

No one should believe in you the way you believe in yourself. When I say visualize your success, I mean *whatever you view as success*. Picture yourself with those things and or people you desire. I'm not just talking about money, because money does not equate to success. Think about what success is to you. Is it a healthy family? Is it having a good job where you can pay all your bills and have money left to save? Is it being able to help your family members who may not have the same resources as you? Is it providing jobs and resources for people in your community?

What is success to you?

Now, visualize it. Visualize everything you desire and whatever you need to do to reach the things you visualized, do it. But you have to visualize it first. The Bible says, where there is no vision, the people perish.

You cannot achieve what you cannot conceive.

I remember getting in the mirror years ago, and I would introduce myself as if I were at an event and act like my biography had been read as a part of my introduction. I could see the crowd and their smiles. I could hear the words people would use to describe me, and as I walked to the podium, I could see it as if I was already there. At the time, I'd done absolutely nothing, and no one really knew my name.

But I knew what I wanted my future to look like.

I knew that the type of work I would do would allow me to be in front of people, speaking and pouring life into them. I believed that it was attainable for me. This is the type of visualization I'm talking about. What I love about these types of visualizations is that no one can take them away from you. Your vision is just that, *yours*, and there's nothing anyone can do about it.

It's yours because it was given to you by God.

What would you do differently if you knew that your gift would make room for you regardless of who's doing it and how many people are doing it? What would you do differently if you knew that regardless of this, you would still be successful and that you would be considered one of the best to ever do it?

Proverbs 18:16 explains that, "A gift opens the way and ushers the giver into the presence of the great."

In other words, you don't have to worry about who, what, when, where or why when it comes to your gift because *your gift will make room for you.* These compelling words remind us of how powerful our skills and talents are and how it facilitates opportunities for elevation. It demonstrates that possessing a talent or gift can move you into success and sometimes recognition.

While recognition should never be the goal, I have learned that when people see your heart and the passion you have for purpose, which is found in your gifts, they will show love and support by recognizing you. In essence, think of your gifts as a bridge. A bridge that leads you over to connections, influence, and impact. Remember, transcending is more about others and less about you. Your ability to help others is what makes you a transcender. I always tell people; you can always find your gifts in the betterment of others. Who have you helped lately? In helping others, you'll also help yourself. It's the blessing that keeps on giving.

I can remember back in the year of 2020 right before I birthed Be THAT. One of the things I was so concerned about was the fact that so many people were 'doing empowerment'. Every time I turned around, someone was becoming a coach or creating a service to empower others. There were so many people doing this that I was reluctant to even start my business. But I had a friend who said to me "Roneisha, there's a church on every corner but does that mean that there isn't a need for more churches?" I thought about that statement and realized that there was so much purpose in my vision, I had to do it.

Can I tell you that birthing a business to empower others has been one of the best and most fulfilling decisions I've ever made? The lives I have been able to touch have been amazing. The rooms I've been invited into have left me emotionally speechless, and the people I've been able to connect with have left me inspired to say the least. And what I love about all of this is that God isn't even done blessing me and He's not done blessing you either. In essence, your gift paves the way to your destiny and I can't wait for you to see what God has for you, your best is yet to come.

> Remember, **Being THAT** doesn't mean you're perfect; it simply means you are purposed and destined for greatness.

I mean think about it, how many of the people you consider to be great were perfect?

Nobody!

Being THAT means that you recognize your flaws and still believe that God can use you. It means that you use your life as motivation for the betterment of others and it means that you embrace every aspect of who you essentially are. Whether you need to start again, pick up where you left off, need encouragement or whether you feel like you are on the very top of your game you can still thrive, hope, affirm, and transcend; you can still Be THAT.

It's impossible to thrive, hope, affirm, and transcend without incorporating God's love. We must remember that God is the reason that we can Be THAT in all that we are and all that we do. Having the presence of God enhances our ability to thrive, hope, affirm, and transcend. Having a relationship with him helps us to see what He sees for our lives. One thing I've learned is that we cannot do life by ourselves. We have an anchor that guides and directs us beyond our now and is unexplainably gracious and rich in God's love. He gives us the power we need to survive.

May we all have the same type of love for ourselves that God has for us. May we all have the Power to Be THAT!

AS YOU CONTINUE TO AFFIRM, REPEAT THE FOLLOWING WORDS FROM YOUR

BE *that!* AFFIRMATION

I will **THRIVE** no matter what yesterday was or what today brings. I will have the audacity to **HOPE** because faith is the assurance of things hoped for. I will **AFFIRM** who I am in God daily and I will **TRANSCEND** beyond my own limitations, because I am capable, I am favored, I am loved, and I am supported. I have the power to **Be THAT!** I have the power to **Be THAT!**

CHAPTER FIVE - BE TRANSCENDING (S) (M) (T) (W) (T) (F) (S)

DATE:

Reflect on your current state of being and consider whether there are areas of your life where you feel limited. How do you perceive the concept of transcending these limitations? Describe any recent experiences or observations that have influenced your understanding of transcending.

Take a moment to identify personal limitations that you feel are holding you back from reaching your full potential. This could include limiting beliefs, fears, societal expectations, reflect on how these limitations impact your sense of purpose.

Envision what transcending these limitations would look like for you. What does it mean to transcend, and what would it feel like to live a life free from the constraints that currently hold you back?

Consider the challenges you may encounter on the path to transcending limitations. How do you plan to navigate these challenges and persevere in your journey?

NOTES / REMINDERS

NOTES / REMINDERS

NOTES / REMINDERS

www.ingramcontent.com/pod-product-compliance
Lightning Source LLC
Chambersburg PA
CBHW071103120626
46546CB00003B/1263